Doggy

Boxers

MARGARET MINCKS

BLACK
RABBIT
BOOKS

Bolt is published by Black Rabbit Books
P.O. Box 3263, Mankato, Minnesota, 56002.
www.blackrabbitbooks.com
Copyright © 2018 Black Rabbit Books

Jennifer Besel, editor; Grant Gould, interior
designer; Michael Sellner, cover designer;
Omay Ayres, photo researcher

Library of Congress Cataloging-in-Publication Data
Names: Mincks, Margaret, author.
Title: Boxers / by Margaret Mincks.
Description: Mankato, Minnesota : Black Rabbit Books, [2018] | Series:
Bolt. Doggie data | Audience: Ages 9-12. | Audience: Grades 4 to 6. |
Includes bibliographical references and index.
Identifiers: LCCN 2016049971 (print) | LCCN 2017003482 (ebook) | ISBN
9781680721492 (library binding) | ISBN 9781680722130 (e-book) | ISBN
9781680724523 (paperback)
Subjects: LCSH: Boxer (Dog breed)–Juvenile literature.
Classification: LCC SF429.B75 M56 2018 (print) | LCC SF429.B75 (ebook)
| DDC 636.73–dc23
LC record available at https://lccn.loc.gov/2016049971

Printed in the United States at CG Book Printers,
North Mankato, Minnesota, 56003. 3/17

Contents

CHAPTER 1

Meet the

The boxer hears its owner drive up. In a flash, it picks up its ball. It races to the gate and spins in circles. Finally, the gate opens. Its owner is home!

The boxer bats the ball to its owner. The dog hops on its back legs, ready to play.

Playful Pup

Boxers are **muscular**, medium-sized dogs. They are strong and **loyal** dogs. But they are also playful. Fun-loving boxers will do anything for a laugh.

How Big Is a Boxer?

HEIGHT
at shoulder
21.5 TO 25 INCHES
(55 to 64 centimeters)

WEIGHT

50 TO 80 POUNDS
(23 to 36 kilograms)

40 50 60
30 70
20 80
10 90
0 100
pounds pounds

PARTS OF A BOXER

EAR

MUZZLE

WRINKLED FOREHEAD

BROWN EYES

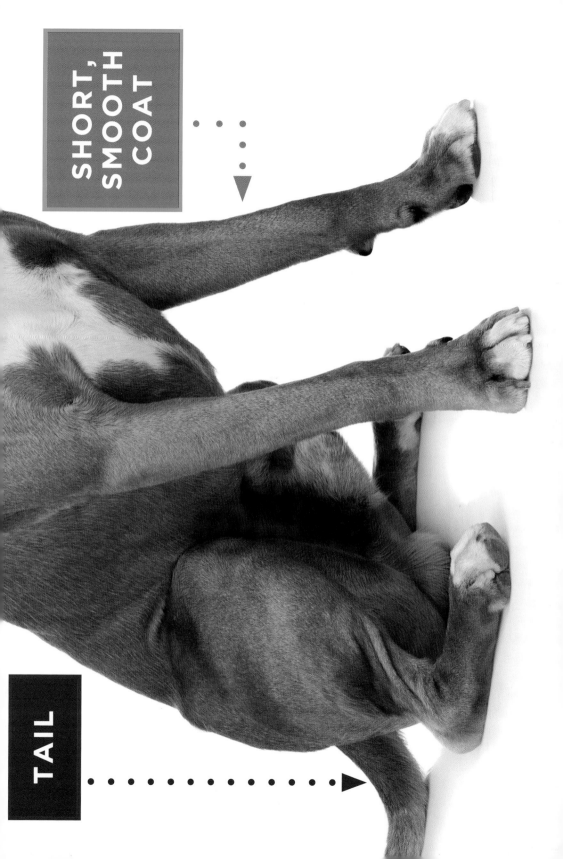

SHORT, SMOOTH COAT

TAIL

CHAPTER 2

A Special

Anytime is playtime for boxers. These dogs often have puppylike energy even as adults. Boxers love attention. They also need plenty of activity.

• • • • • • • • • • • • • • • • • • • •

Boxers like to clown around. They hop, dance, and spin in circles. They get their name from the "boxing" they do with their paws.

Protective Partner

Boxers are loyal and **protective** of their owners. They make great watchdogs and guard dogs. They bark only when they sense danger.

TOP 10 MOST POPULAR Dogs in the United States in 2015

1	2	3	4
Labrador Retrievers	German Shepherds	Golden Retrievers	Bulldogs

5	6	7	8	9	10
Beagles	French Bulldogs	Yorkshire Terriers	Poodles	Rottweilers	Boxers

Boxer Challenges

Boxers love their owners. They usually get along with other pets too. But some might try to chase cats.

Boxers can be **stubborn** too. They are very smart, but they get bored easily. Training this **breed** can be tough.

Boxers drool and snore a lot.

CHAPTER 3

Boxers' Features

Boxers are **sleek** and sporty. Their short, smooth coats can be tan, brick red, or striped with white markings.

Boxers' ears naturally hang down. Sometimes breeders **crop** the ears. They do this to give the dogs a certain look. Sometimes breeders also **dock** boxers' tails.

**25.5 TO 30 INCHES
(65 TO 76 CM)**

COMPARING
SIZES

SAINT
BERNARD

140 to 200
POUNDS
(64 to 90 kg)

Boxer Health

Boxers are fairly healthy dogs. But some do have health problems. This breed may suffer from cancer, heart issues, and bloat. Bloat happens when a dog's stomach twists. Food, water, and air get trapped inside.

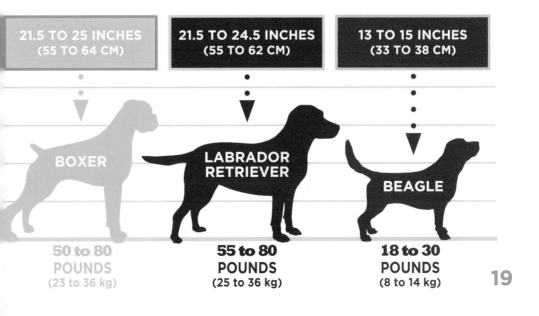

21.5 TO 25 INCHES
(55 TO 64 CM)

21.5 TO 24.5 INCHES
(55 TO 62 CM)

13 TO 15 INCHES
(33 TO 38 CM)

BOXER

LABRADOR RETRIEVER

BEAGLE

50 to 80 POUNDS (23 to 36 kg)

55 to 80 POUNDS (25 to 36 kg)

18 to 30 POUNDS (8 to 14 kg)

Boxer Life Cycle

Newborn boxers weigh about 1 pound (.5 kg).

PUPPY

Boxers become seniors at around seven years old. Senior boxers move more slowly and sleep more.

ADOLESCENT

Between six months and one year, boxers grow a lot.

ADULT

Most boxers are fully grown by their second birthdays.

SENIOR

CHAPTER 4

Caring for Boxers

All dogs need regular vet checkups. They also need care at home. Boxers aren't hard to groom. Their smooth, short coats only need a weekly brushing. They need baths when they get dirty. They also need their nails trimmed. Owners should also brush their boxers' teeth a few times a week.

Boxers live
between
10 and
12 years.

Eating and Exercising

Feeding boxers can be expensive. These dogs eat more food than smaller breeds. Boxers shouldn't be allowed to gulp their food down fast. Eating fast can cause bloat.

Boxers need serious exercise. They should have regular walks and playtime. Adult boxers make great hiking and jogging buddies.

Boxers can be trained to help police find missing people. Boxers also make excellent service dogs for deaf and blind people.

Loyal and Full of Energy

Boxers are friendly, funny, and full of energy. These loyal canines make great pets. But you have to keep up with them!

A boxer holds the record for world's longest dog tongue. Its tongue was 17 inches (43 cm) long!

Is a Boxer

Answer the questions below. Then add up your points to see if a boxer is a good fit.

1 What's your energy level?

A. I'm very active. **(3 points)**

B. It depends on the day. **(2 points)**

C. Napping is my favorite sport. **(1 point)**

2 What's your favorite size for an adult dog?

A. medium to large (3 points)

B. extra large (2 points)

C. teeny-tiny (1 point)

3 What do you think of the puppy stage?

A. It's cute and hilarious! (3 points)

B. It's sometimes fun and sometimes annoying. (2 points)

C. I prefer when dogs get older and chill out. (1 point)

{
3 points
A boxer is not your best match.
4–8 points
You like boxers, but another breed might be better for you.
9 points
A sporty boxer could be your best buddy!
}

GLOSSARY

adolescent (ad-oh-LES-uhnt)—a young person or animal that is developing into an adult

breed (BREED)—a particular kind of dog, cat, horse, or other animal

crop (KRAHP)—to cut off the upper or outer parts of something

dock (DAHK)—to cut off the end of a tail

loyal (LOY-uhl)—having complete support for someone or something

muscular (MUS-kyu-lur)—having large and strong muscles

muzzle (MUH-zuhl)—the usually long nose and mouth of an animal

protective (pro-TEK-tiv)—keeping someone or something from being harmed

sleek (SLEEK)—straight and smooth

stubborn (STUH-bern)—refusing to start or stop doing something

BOOKS

Gaines, Ann Graham. *Top 10 Dogs for Kids.* American Humane Association Top 10 Pets for Kids. Berkeley Heights, NJ: Enslow Elementary an imprint of Enslow Publishers, Inc., 2015.

Johnson, Jinny. *Boxer.* My Favorite Dog. Mankato, MN: Smart Apple Media, 2013.

Schuh, Mari. *Boxers.* Awesome Dogs. Minneapolis: Bellwether Media, 2016.

WEBSITES

American Boxer Club
americanboxerclub.org

Boxer
www.akc.org/dog-breeds/boxer/

Pets: Taking Care of Your Pet
pbskids.org/itsmylife/family/pets/article7.html

INDEX